HOW TO WRITE
IN
PERSIAN

(A Workbook for Learning the Persian Alphabet)

Nazanin Mirsadeghi

Bahar Books

www.baharbooks.com

Mirsadeghi, Nazanin
    How to Write in Persian: A Workbook for Learning the Persian Alphabet (Farsi-English Bi-lingual Edition)/
Nazanin Mirsadeghi

ISBN-10: 1939099471
ISBN-13: 978-1-939099-47-1

Published by Bahar Books, White Plains, New York

Contents

Introduction

This workbook is designed for use by non-native learners of the Persian language. It is intended for beginners who seek to learn the Persian alphabet and script.

By using visual directions and exercises, the workbook will help the reader overcome some of the difficulties associated with the process of learning the Persian script. Before you start using this book, it is strongly recommended that you review the table provided at the beginning of the book containing a brief guide to the pronunciation of the Persian letters. This will enable you to sound out the letters and words as you advance through the chapters and exercises. This book will provide you with a clear description for each Persian letter, including its name, sound and forms. Examples for various forms of each letter are also given to facilitate the learning process. Visual directions for writing each letter are then followed by exercises which enhance your Persian writing skills.

After covering all the Persian letters, the workbook offers the opportunity to practice writing Persian words. It also contains instructions for writing Persian numbers, samples of common Persian fonts and examples of typical Persian handwriting styles.

All of the examples of the Persian words used in this book are accompanied by their English translations and the transliterations of the Persian words.

It is hoped that this workbook will help those interested in learning the Persian script and improve their applied knowledge of the Persian language.

THE
PERSIAN ALPHABET

FACTS:

1. There are 32 letters and 3 Arabic signs in the Persian alphabet.

2. In addition to the letters, there are 3 short vowels, and 3 long vowels some of which share their shapes with specific letters.

3. Short vowels are usually omitted in writing.

4. Long vowels are not omitted in writing.

5. The Persian script is written from right to left.

6. There are no capital letters in Persian.

7. Each letter joins the letter preceding it and the letter following it; However, there is a group of letters that only join another letter from their right and never from their left. This group consists of these 7 letters:

آ-ا , د , ذ , ر , ز , ژ and و .

List of the Persian Letters

1. ‏آ – ا‏	9. ‏خ – خـ‏	17. ‏ص – صـ‏	25. ‏ک – ک‏
2. ‏ب – بـ‏	10. ‏د‏	18. ‏ض – ضـ‏	26. ‏گ – گ‏
3. ‏پ – پـ‏	11. ‏ذ‏	19. ‏ط‏	27. ‏ل – لـ‏
4. ‏ت – تـ‏	12. ‏ر‏	20. ‏ظ‏	28. ‏م – مـ‏
5. ‏ث – ثـ‏	13. ‏ز‏	21. ‏ع – ـعـ – ـع – عـ‏	29. ‏ن – نـ‏
6. ‏ج – جـ‏	14. ‏ژ‏	22. ‏غ – ـغـ – ـغ – غـ‏	30. ‏و‏
7. ‏چ – چـ‏	15. ‏س – سـ‏	23. ‏ف – فـ‏	31. ‏ه – ـه – ـهـ – هـ‏
8. ‏ح – حـ‏	16. ‏ش – شـ‏	24. ‏ق – قـ‏	32. ‏ی – یـ‏

Important Notes:

1. Before starting to use this book, review the table on page 9 thoroughly, to familiarize yourself with the pronunciation of the Persian letters.

2. Keep in mind that in Persian you write from right to left.

3. Then, start writing each letter by following the visual directions, progressing from right to left.

4. Move your pen in the directions shown by the arrows to reach the final point of each letter.

5. Dots and strokes are essential elements of the letters; therefore, you can not skip writing the dots or strokes.

6. Write the dots last. Place them where they belong after writing other parts of the letter.

7. Pay special attention to the position of the dots and the number of dots; these two factors are your only tools for distinguishing some letters from others.

8. Practice writing each letter, number or word as many times as you need in the spaces provided.

Summary of the Pronunciation
of the Persian Letters

ǎ like "a" in arm	آ – ا
b like "b" in ball	بـ – ب
p like "p" in party	پـ – پ
t like "t" in time	تـ – ت
s like "s" in sun	ثـ – ث
j like "j" in jam	جـ – ج
č like "ch" in chair	چـ – چ
h like "h" in happy	حـ – ح
ǩ like "ch" in the German word *bach*, or Hebrew word *smach*.	خـ – خ
d like "d" in door	د
z like "z" in zoo	ذ
r like "r" in red	ر
z like "z" in zoo	ز
ž like the "z" in Zwago	ژ
s like "s" in sun	سـ – س
š like "sh" in she	شـ – ش
s like "s" in sun	صـ – ص
z like "z" in zoo	ضـ – ض
t like "t" in time	ط
z like "z" in zoo	ظ
' is a glottal stop, like between the syllables of "uh-oh"	عـ – ـعـ – ـع – ع
ǧ like "r" in the French word *merci*	غـ – ـغـ – ـغ – غ

f like "f" in fall	فـ – ف
ǧ like "r" in the French word *merci*	قـ – ق
k like "k" in kite	کـ – ک
g like "g" in game	گـ – گ
l like "l" in love	لـ – ل
m like "m" in mother	مـ – م
n like "n" in name	نـ – ن
v like "v" in van	و
h like "h" in happy	هـ – ـهـ – ـه – ه
y like the "y" in yellow	یـ – ی

Short Vowels

a like the "a" in apple	ـَ – اَ
o like the "o" in ocean	ـُ – اُ
e like the "e" in egg	ـِ – اِ

Long Vowels

ǎ like "a" in arm	آ – ا
u like the "oo" in root	او – و
e like the "ee" in seed	ایـ – یـ – ای-ی

Arabic Signs

Represents doubled consonants.	ّ
' is a glottal stop, like between the syllables of "uh-oh"	ء
an like "an" in "can"	ً

/ă/

Name: ‏الف‎ أ /a.lef/

Sound: This letter sounds like the letter "a" in the word **arm**.

Forms: This letter has two forms: ‏ا‎ – آ

- " آ " is used in the beginning of a word.

Example:

beginning: ‏آب‎ /ăb/ (water)

- " ا " is used in the middle or at the end of a word.

Examples:

middle: ‏باد‎ /băd/ (wind)

end: ‏صدا‎ /se.dă/ (sound), ‏ما‎ /mă/ (we)

Keep in Mind: This letter only joins the letter preceding it and never the letter following it.

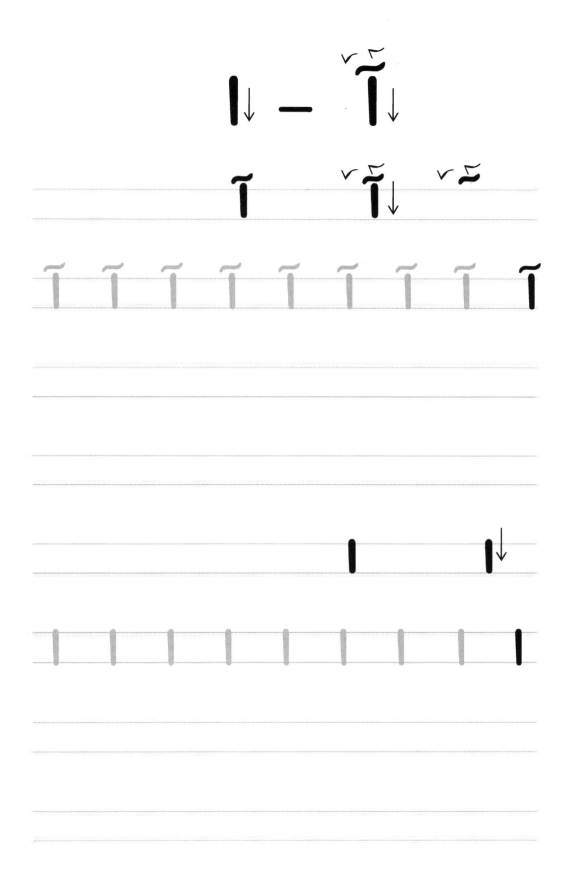

/b/

Name: بِ /be/

Sound: This letter sounds like the letter "b" in the word **ball**.

Forms: This letter has two forms: ب - بـ

- "بـ" is used in the beginning or the middle of a word.

Examples:

beginning: باد /băd/ (wind)

middle: مبل /mobl/ (sofa), آبی /ă.bi/ (blue)

- "ب" is used at the end of a word.

Examples:

end: شب /šab/ (night), کتاب /ke.tăb/ (book)

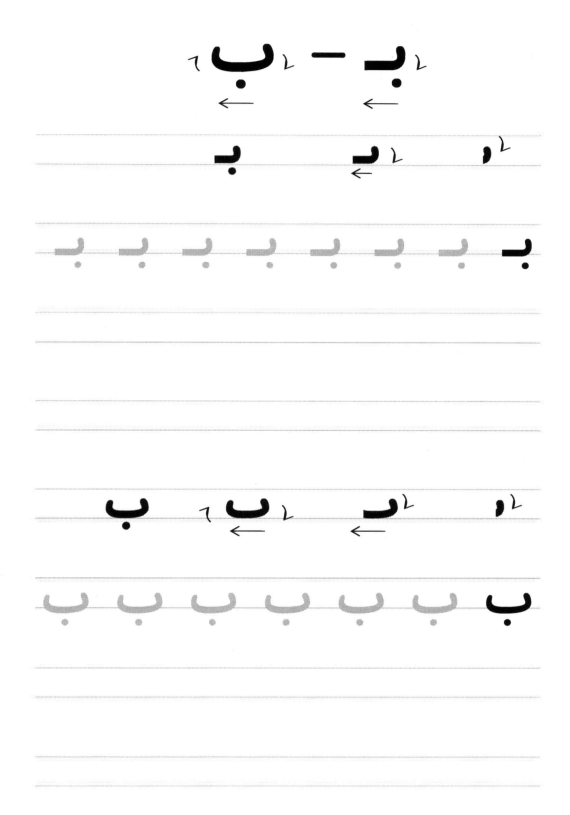

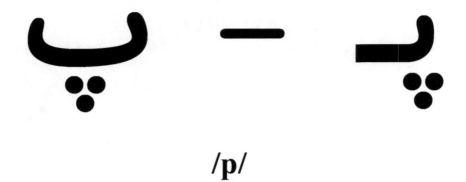

/p/

Name: پ /pe/

Sound: This letter sounds like the letter "p" in the word **party**.

Forms: This letter has two forms: پ - ﭗ

- "ﭘ" is used in the beginning or the middle of a word.

Examples:

beginning: پدر /pe.dar/ (father)

middle: آپارتمان / ă.păr.te.măn/ (apartment), آبپاش /ăb.păš/ (watering can)

- "پ" is used at the end of a word.

Examples:

end: لامپ /lămp/ (bulb), سوپ / sup/ (soup)

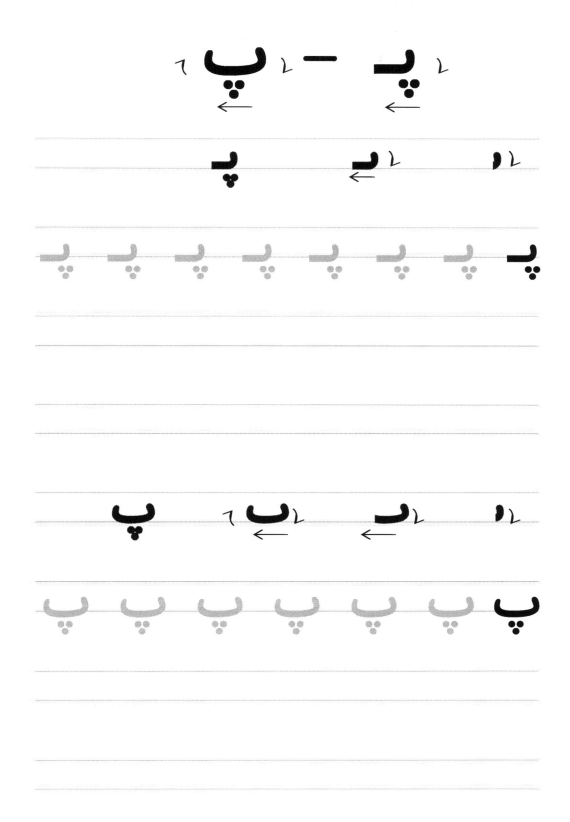

/t/

Name: ت ‎/te/

Sound: This letter sounds like the letter "t" in the word **time**.

Forms: This letter has two forms: ت ‏- ‏تـ

- "تـ" is used in the beginning or the middle of a word.

Examples:

beginning: تماشا ‎/ta.mǎ.šǎ/ (viewing)

middle: اتاق ‎/o.tǎğ/ (room),   شتر ‎/šo.tor/ (camel)

- "ت" is used at the end of a word.

Examples:

end: دست ‎/dast/ (hand),   حیوانات ‎/hey.vǎ.nǎt/ (animals)

16

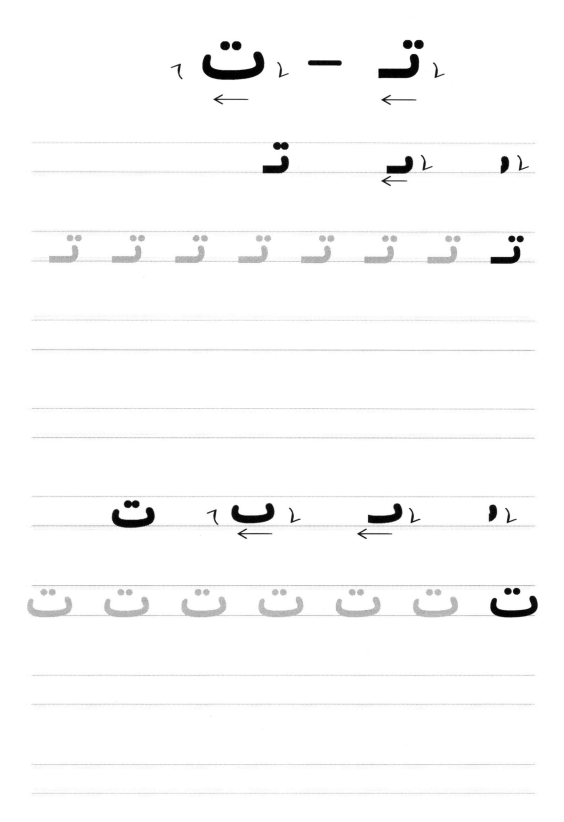

/s/

Name: ثِ /se/

Sound: This letter sounds like the letter "s" in the word **sand**.

Forms: This letter has two forms: ث - ث

- "ث" is used in the beginning or the middle of a word.

Examples:

  beginning: ثانیه /sǎ.ni.ye/ (second)

  middle: مثبت /mos.bat/ (positive) , مرثیه /mar.si.ye/ (elegy)

- "ث" is used at the end of a word.

Examples:

  end: بحث /bahs/ (discussion), احداث /eh.dǎs/ (construction)

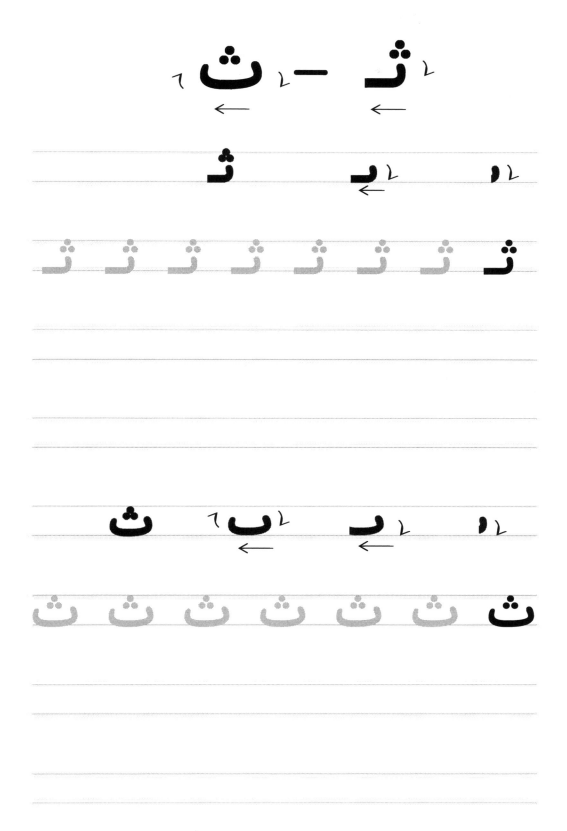

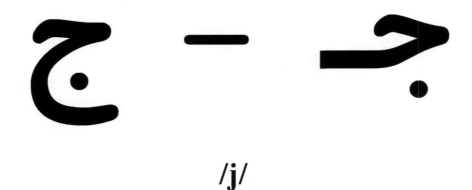

/j/

Name: جیم /jim/

Sound: This letter sounds like the letter "j" in the word **jam**.

Forms: This letter has two forms: ج - جـ

- "جـ" is used in the beginning or the middle of a word.

Examples:

beginning: جنگ /jang/ (war)

middle: تجارت /te.jă.rat/ (commerce), اجرا /ej.ră/ (performance)

- "ج" is used at the end of a word.

Examples:

end: کج /kaj/ (tilted), کاج /kăj/ (pine)

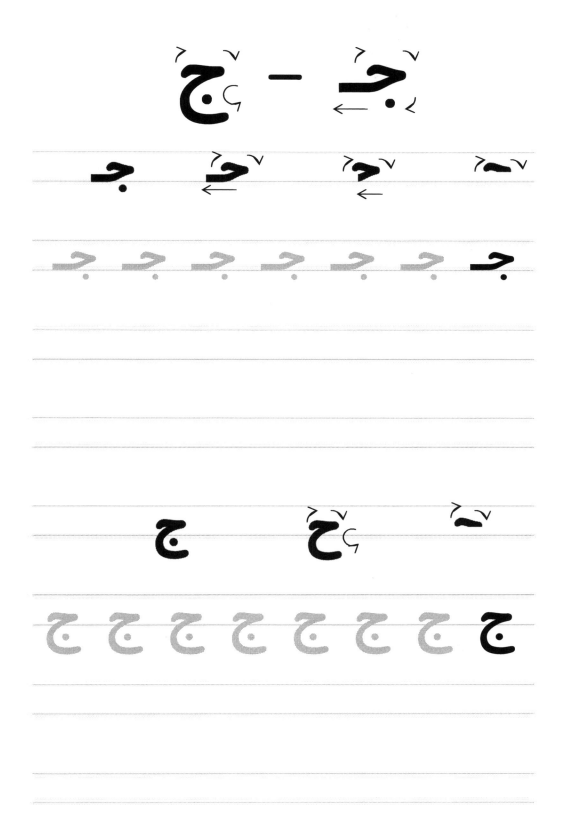

/č/

Name: چ /če/

Sound: This letter sounds like "ch" in the word **chair**.

Forms: This letter has two forms: چ - چ

- "چ" is used in the beginning or the middle of a word.

Examples:

  beginning: چرخ /čarǩ/ (wheel)

  middle: کوچه /ku.če/ (alley), بچّه /bač.če/ (child)

- "چ" is used at the end of a word.

Examples:

  end: گچ /gač/ (chalk), ماچ /mǎč/ (kiss)

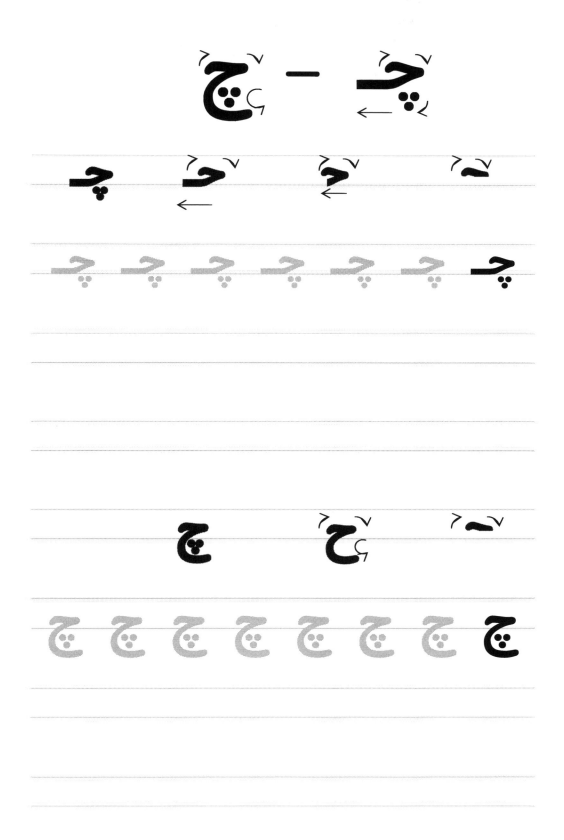

/h/

Name: حِ /he/

Sound: This letter sounds like the letter "h" in the word **happy**.

Forms: This letter has two forms: ح - حـ

- "حـ" is used in the beginning or the middle of a word.

Examples:

beginning: حلق /halğ/(throat)

middle: صحنه /sah.ne/(stage), احساس /eh.săs/(feeling)

- "ح" is used at the end of a word.

Examples:

end: صلح /solh/(peace), اصلاح /es.lăh/(correction)

ح – ح

ح   ح   ح   ح

ح ح ح ح ح ح ح ح

ح   ح   ح

ح ح ح ح ح ح ح ح

/ǩ/

Name: خِ /ǩe/

Sound: This letter sounds like "ch" in the German word **"bach"** or the Hebrew word **"smach"**.

Forms: This letter has two forms: خ – خـ

- "خـ" is used in the beginning or the middle of a word.

Examples:

beginning: خانم /ǩǎ.nom/ (lady)

middle: دختر /doǩ.tar/ (daughter/girl), تخت /taǩt/ (bed)

- "خ" is used at the end of a word.

Examples:

end: یخ /yaǩ/ (ice), سرخ /sorǩ/ (red)

/d/

Name: دال /dăl/

Sound: This letter sounds like the letter "d" in the word **door**.

Forms: This letter has one form: د

- "د" is used in the beginning, the middle or at the end of a word.

Examples:

beginning: دست /dast/(hand)

middle: گندم /gan.dom/(wheat), شادی /šă.di/(happiness/joy)

end: بد /bad/(bad), مرد /mard/(man)

Keep in Mind: This letter only joins the letter preceding it and never the letter following it.

/z/

Name: ذال /zăl/

Sound: This letter sounds like the letter "z" in the word **zoo**.

Forms: This letter has one form: ذ

- "ذ" is used in the beginning, the middle or at the end of a word.

Examples:

beginning: ذرّت /zor.rat/(corn)

middle: تغذیه /tağ.zi.ye/(nutrition), آذر /ă.zar/(December)

end: کاغذ /kă.ğaz/(paper)

Keep in Mind: This letter only joins the letter preceding it and never the letter following it.

ذ ذ ذ ذ ذ ذ ذ ذ ذ ذ

/r/

Name: رِ /re/

Sound: This letter sounds like the letter "r" in the word **red**.

Forms: This letter has one form: ر

- "ر" is used in the beginning, the middle or at the end of a word.

Examples:

beginning: روز /ruz/ (day)

middle: مرد /mard/ (man), آرام /ă.răm/ (slow)

end: پسر /pe.sar/ (son/boy), کار /kăr/ (work)

Keep in Mind: This letter only joins the letter preceding it and never the letter following it.

/z/

Name: زِ /ze/

Sound: This letter sounds like the letter "z" in the word **zoo**.

Forms: This letter has one form: ز

- "ز" is used in the beginning, the middle or at the end of a word.

Examples:

beginning: زرد /zard/ (yellow)

middle: موزیک /mu.zik/ (music), بزرگ /bo.zorg/ (big)

end: راز /răz/ (secret), سرسبز /sar.sabz/ (freshly green)

Keep in Mind: This letter only joins the letter preceding it and never the letter following it.

ز

ز ز

ز ز ز ز ز ز ز ز ز

/ž/

Name: ژ /že/

Sound: This letter sounds like the letter "z" in the word **zwago**.

Forms: This letter has one form: ژ

- "ژ" is used in the beginning, the middle or at the end of a word.

Examples:

beginning: ژاکت /žǎ.kat/ (cardigan)

middle: اژدها /ež.de.hǎ/ (dragon), مژه /mo.že/ (eye-lash)

end: کژ /kaž/ (tilted), شوفاژ /šu.fǎž/ (radiator)

Keep in Mind: This letter only joins the letter preceding it and never the letter following it.

/s/

Name: سین /sin/

Sound: This letter sounds like the letter "s" in the word **sun**.

Forms: This letter has two forms: س - ‌سـ

- "سـ" is used in the beginning or the middle of a word.

Examples:

beginning: سیب /sib/ (apple)

middle: اسب /asb/(horse), پسر /pe.sar/(son/boy)

- "س" is used at the end of a word.

Examples:

end: مس /mes/ (copper), یاس /yǎs/(jasmine)

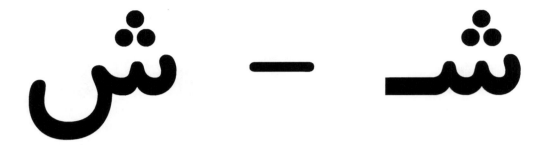

/š/

Name: شین /šin/

Sound: This letter sounds like "sh" in the word **she**.

Forms: This letter has two forms: ش - ﺷ

- "ﺷ" is used in the beginning or the middle of a word.

Examples:

beginning: شما /šo.mǎ/ (you pl.)

middle: اشک /ašk/ (tear), دانشجو /dǎ.neš.ju/ (college student)

- "ش" is used at the end of a word.

Examples:

end: آتش /ǎ.taš/ (fire), تراش /ta.rǎš/ (pencil sharpener)

/s/

Name: صاد /săd/

Sound: This letter sounds like the letter "s" in the word **sun**.

Forms: This letter has two forms: ص - صـ

- "صـ" is used in the beginning or at the middle of a word.

Examples:

beginning: صدف /sa.daf/(shell)

middle: اصل /asl/(origin), خصوصى /ǩo.su.si/(private)

- "ص" is used at the end of a word.

Examples:

end: خاص /ǩăs/(special), خالص /ǩă.les/(pure)

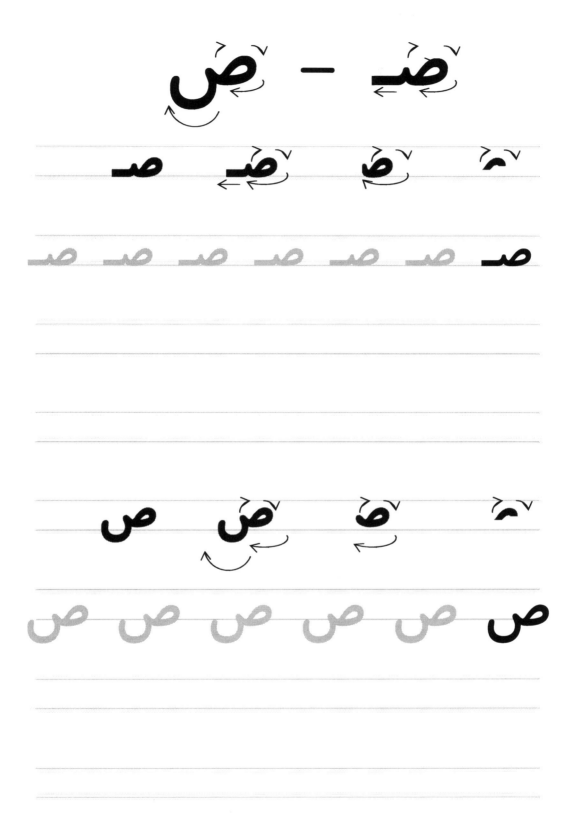

/z/

Name: ضاد /zăd/

Sound: This letter sounds like the letter "z" in the word **zoo**.

Forms: This letter has two forms: ض – ضـ

- "ضـ" is used in the beginning or at the middle of a word.

Examples:

beginning: ضمیمه /za.mi.me/ (attachment)

middle: مضمون /maz.mun/ (content),   واضح /vă.zeh/ (clear)

- "ض" is used at the end of a word.

Examples:

end: مرض /ma.raz/ (sickness),   مریض /ma.riz/ (sick)

/t/

Name: ط /tă/

Sound: This letter sounds like the letter "t" in the word **time**.

Forms: This letter has one form: ط

- "ط" is used in the beginning, the middle or at the end of a word.

Examples:

beginning: طبل /tabl/(drum)

middle: قطره /ğat.re/(drop), اطاعت /e.tă.'at/(obedience)

end: خط /ǩat/(script), نشاط /ne.šăt/(happiness/joy)

/z/

Name: ظ /zǎ/

Sound: This letter sounds like the letter "z" in the word **zoo**.

Forms: This letter has one form: ظ

- "ظ" is used in the beginning, the middle or at the end of a word.

Examples:

beginning: ظلم /zolm/ (oppression)

middle: مظهر /maz.har/ (symbol), وظیفه /va.zi.fe/ (task)

end: حفظ /hefz/ (preservation), لحاظ /la.hǎz/ (point of view)

ع - ﻊ - ﻌ - ﻋ

/ʿ/

Name: عِین / ʿeyn/

Sound: This letter represents a glottal stop like between the syllables of **"uh-oh"**.

Forms: This letter has four forms: ع - ﻊ - ﻌ - ﻋ

- "ﻋ" is used in the beginning of a word or in the middle of a word, after one of these 7 letters: ا-آ , د , ذ , ر , ز , ژ or و .
Examples:
  beginning: عربی /ʿa.ra.bi/ (Arabic)
  middle: زعفران /zaʿ.fe.răn/ (saffron)

- "ﻌ" is used in the middle of a word.
Example:
  middle: معلّم /moʿ.al.lem/ (teacher)

- "ﻊ" is used at the end of a word.
Example:
  end: مطّلع /mot.ta.leʿ/ (knowledgeable)

- "ع" is used at the end of a word, after one of these 7 letters:
  ا , د , ذ , ر , ز , ژ or و .
Example:
  end: مجموع /maj.muʿ/ (sum)

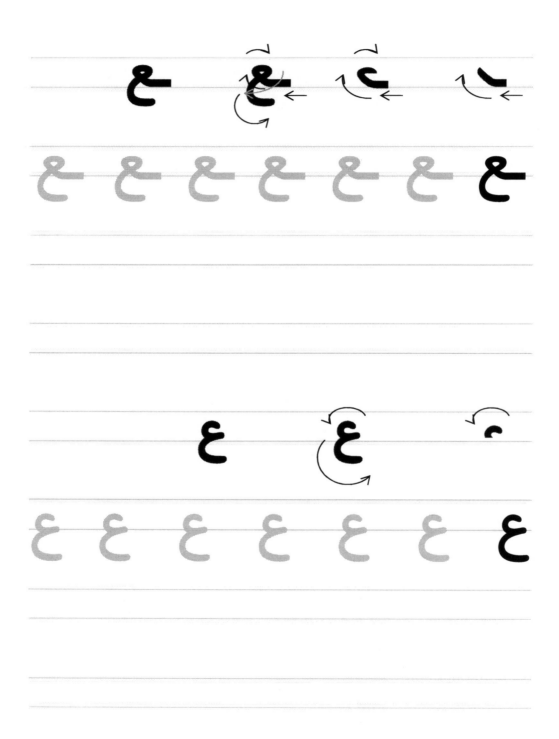

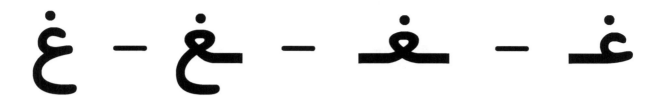

/ğ/

Name: غین /ğeyn/

Sound: This letter sounds like the letter "r" in the French word **"merci"**.

Forms: This letter has four forms: غ - ـغ - ـغـ - غـ

- "غـ" is used in the beginning of a word or in the middle of a word, after one of these 7 letters: آ-ا , د , ذ , ر , ز , ژ or و .

Examples:

beginning: غار /ğăr/ (cave)

middle: آغاز /ă.ğăz/ (beginning)

- "ـغـ" is used in the middle of a word.

Example:

middle: تغییر /tağ.yir/ (change)

- "ـغ" is used at the end of a word.

Example:

end: جیغ /jiğ/ (scream)

- "غ" is used at the end of a word, after one of these 7 letters: ا , د , ذ , ر , ر , ز , ژ or و .

Example:

end: چراغ /če.răğ/ (lamp)

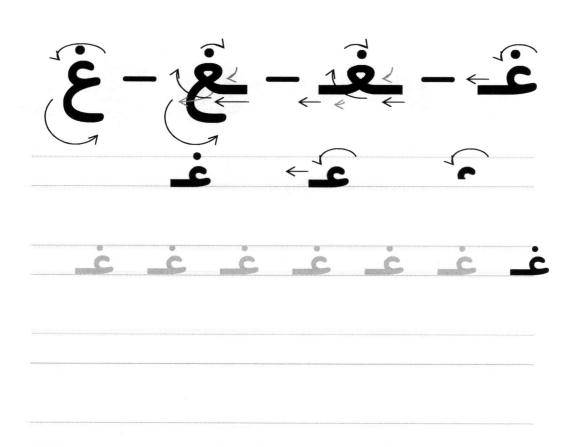

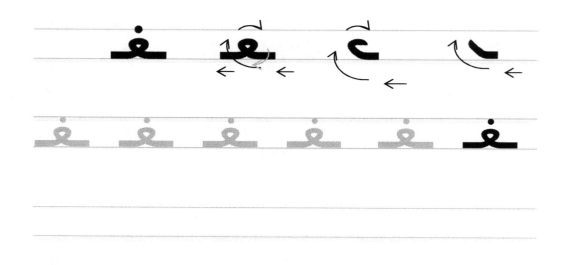

54

/f/

Name: ف /fe/

Sound: This letter sounds like the letter "f" in the word **fall**.

Forms: This letter has two forms: ف - ف

- "ف" is used in the beginning or the middle of a word.

Examples:

   beginning: فارسی /făr.si/ (Persian/Farsi)

   middle: رفتار /raf.tăr/ (behavior),   سفر /sa.far/ (trip)

- "ف" is used at the end of a word.

Examples:

   end: برف /barf/ (snow),   کیف /kif/ (bag)

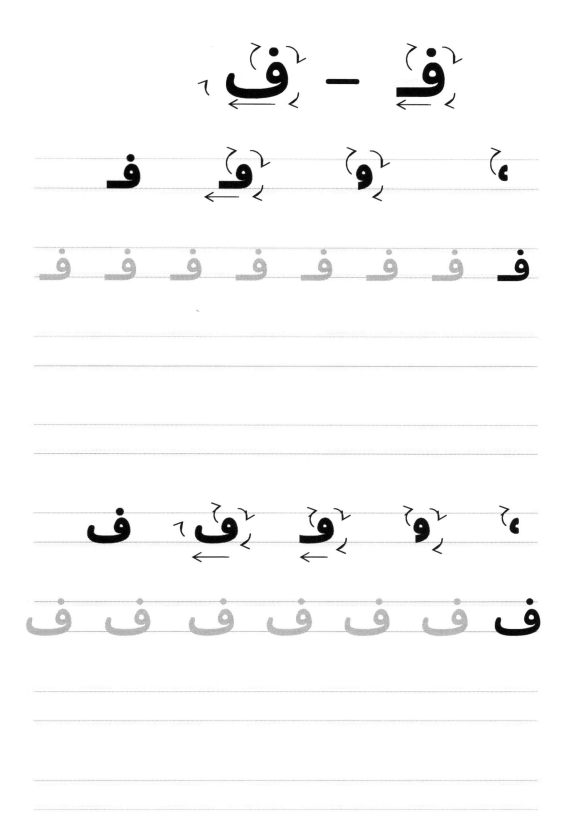

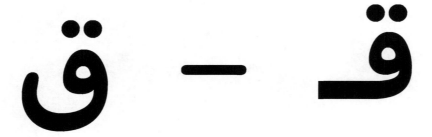

/ğ̆/

Name: قاف /ğ̆ăf/

Sound: This letter sounds like the letter "r" in the French word **"merci"**.

Forms: This letter has two forms: ق – قـ

- "قـ" is used in the beginning or the middle of a word.

Examples:

beginning: قاضی /ğ̆ă.zi/ (judge)

middle: رقص /rağs/ (dance), نقطه /noğ.te/ (dot)

- "ق" is used at the end of a word.

Examples:

end: برق /barğ/ (electricity), عشق /ešğ/ (love)

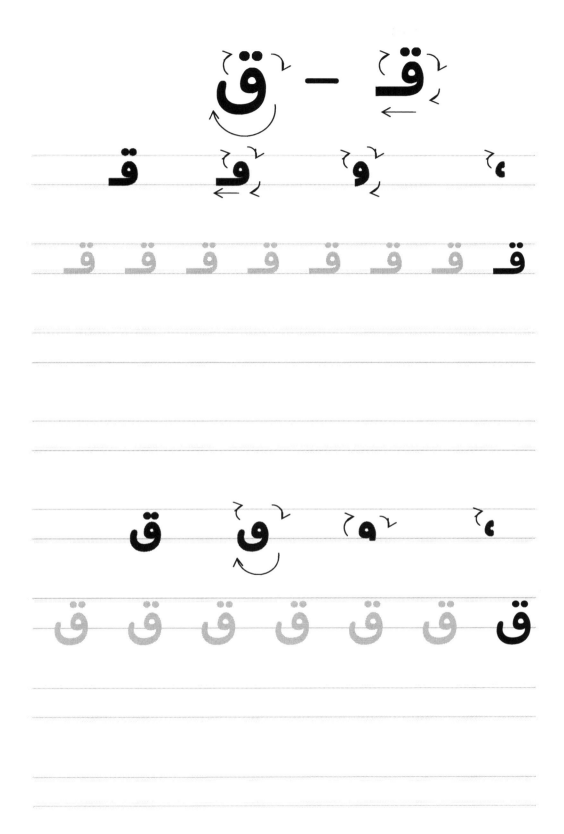

/k/

Name: کاف /kǎf/

Sound: This letter sounds like the letter "k" in the word **kite**.

Forms: This letter has two forms: ک – ک

- "ک" is used in the beginning or the middle of a word.

Examples:

beginning: کتاب /ke.tǎb/ (book)

middle: دکتر /dok.tor/ (doctor),   شکل /šekl/ (shape)

- "ک" is used at the end of a word.

Examples:

end: بادکُنَک /bǎd.ko.nak/ (balloon),   بادبادک /bǎd.bǎ.dak/ (kite)

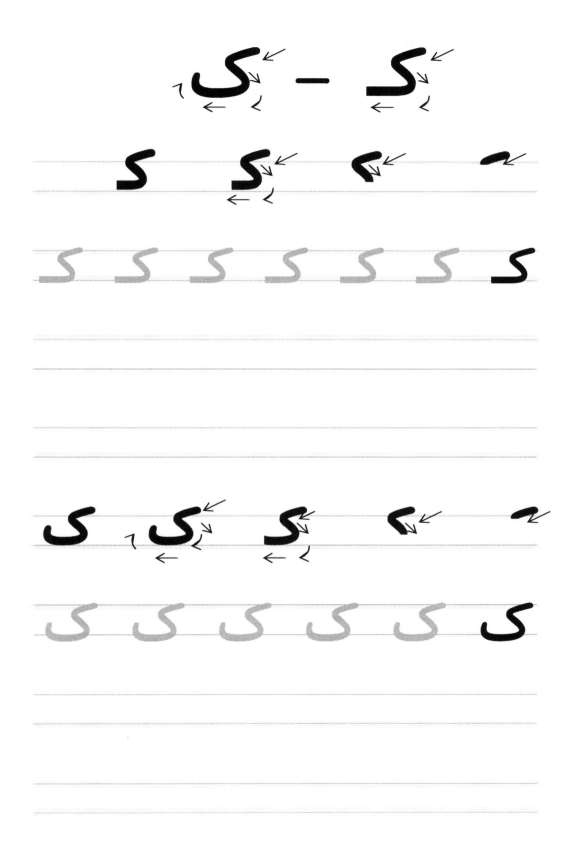

/**g**/

Name: گاف /gǎf/

Sound: This letter sounds like the letter "g" in the word **game**.

Forms: This letter has two forms: گ – گ

- "گ" is used in the beginning or the middle of a word.

Examples:

beginning: گلدان /gol/ (flowerpot)

middle: اگر /a.gar/ (if), انگلیسی /en.ge.li.si/ (English)

- "گ" is used at the end of a word.

Examples:

end: برگ /barg/ (leaf), سنگ /sang/ (stone)

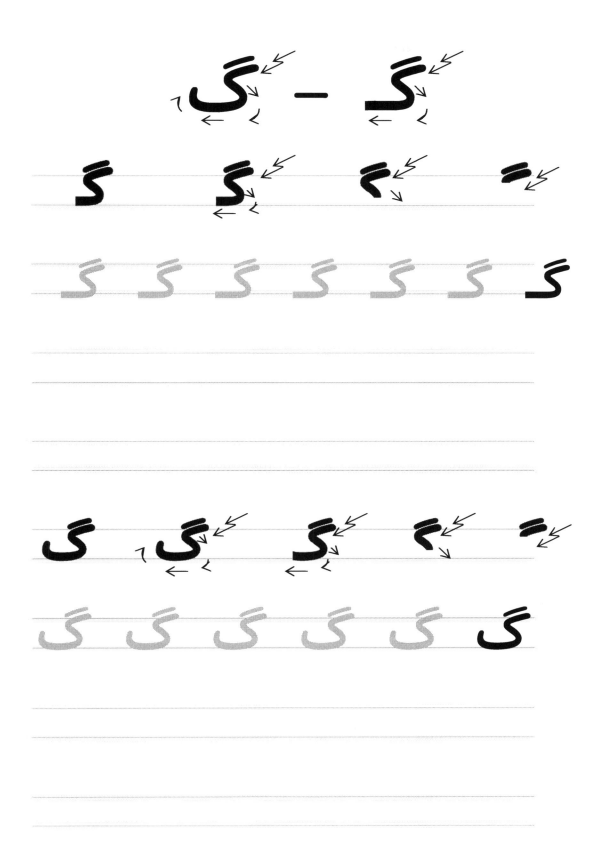

/l/

Name: لام /lăm/

Sound: This letter sounds like the letter "l" in the word **love**.

Forms: This letter has two forms: ل – ل

- " ل " is used in the beginning or in the middle of a word.

Examples:

beginning: ليمو /li.mu/ (lemon/lime)

middle: دليل /da.lil/ (reason), علم /ʿelm/ (science)

- "ل" is used at the end of a word.

Examples:

end: سال /săl/ (year), سیل /seyl/ (flood)

(When the letter ل joins the letter ا , they appear in a specific way: لا)

/m/

Name: میم /mim/

Sound: This letter sounds like the letter "m" in the word **mother**.

Forms: This letter has two forms: مـ – م

- "مـ" is used in the beginning or the middle of a word.

Examples:

beginning: من /man/ (I)

middle: آرامش /ă.ră.meš/ (calmness), همیشه /ha.mi.še/ (forever/always)

- "م" is used at the end of a word.

Examples:

end: لازم /lă.zem/ (necessary), سهم /sahm/ (share)

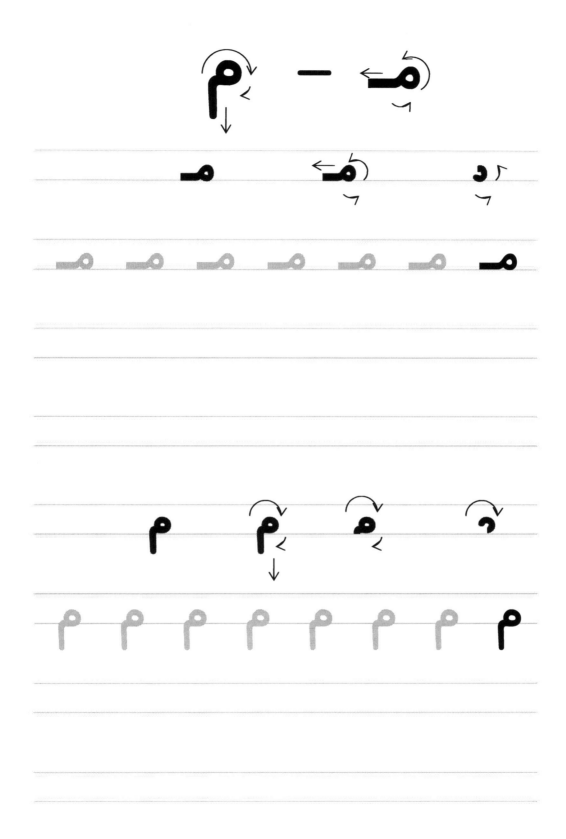

/n/

Name: نون /nun/

Sound: This letter sounds like the letter "n" in the word **name**.

Forms: This letter has two forms: ن - نـ

- " نـ " is used in the beginning or the middle of a word.

Examples:

  beginning: نمره /nom.re/ (number/grade)

  middle: انار /a.năr/ (pomegranate), طناب /ta.năb/ (rope)

- " ن " is used at the end of a word.

Examples:

  end: شاهین /šă.hin/ (falcon), زمان /za.măn/ (time)

و

/v/

Name: واو /văv/

Sound: This letter sounds like the letter "v" in the word **van**.

Forms: This letter has one form: و

- "و" is used in the beginning, the middle or at the end of a word.

Examples:

beginning: ورزش /var.zeš/ (sport)

middle: جوان /ja.văn/ (young), دونده /da.van.de/ (runner)

end: جوّ /javv/ (atmosphere), گاو /găv/ (cow)

Keep in Mind: This letter only joins the letter preceding it and never the letter following it.

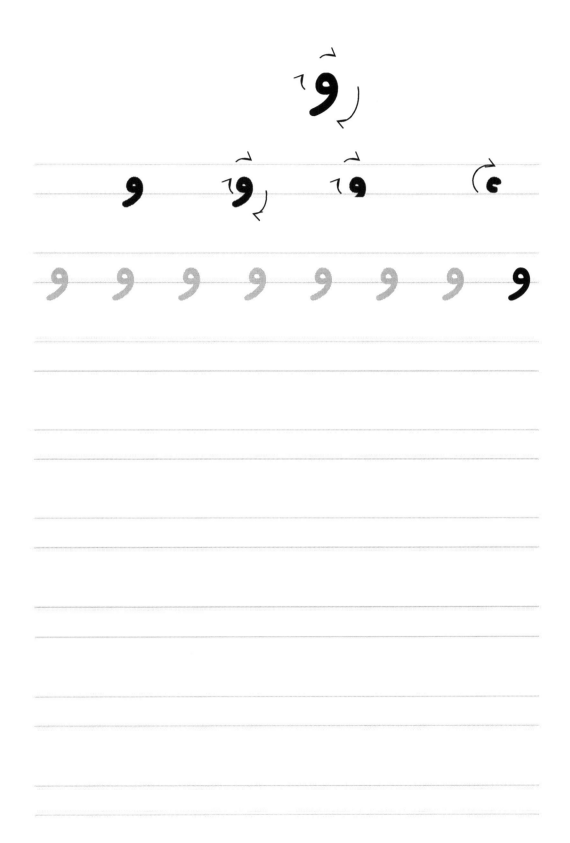

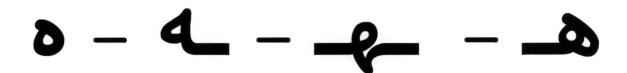

/h/

Name: ‎ه‎ /he/

Sound: This letter sounds like the letter "h" in the word **happy**.

Forms: This letter has four forms: ‎ه - ـه - ـهـ - هـ‎

- "‎هـ‎" is used in the beginning of a word, or in the middle of a word, after one of these 7 letters: ‎آ-ا , د , ذ , ر , ز , ژ‎ or ‎و‎ .

Examples:

beginning: ‎هرگز‎ /har.gez/ (never)

middle: ‎گاهی‎ /gă.hi/ (sometimes)

- "‎ـهـ‎" is used in the middle of a word.

Example:

middle: ‎سهم‎ /sahm/ (share)

- "‎ـه‎" is used at the end of a word.

Example:

end: ‎نُه‎ /noh/ (nine)

- "‎ه‎" is used at the end of a word, after one of these 7 letters: ‎ا , د , ذ , ر , ز , ژ‎ or ‎و‎ .

Example:

end: ‎دانشگاه‎ /dă.neš.găh/ (university)

/y/

Name: یِ /ye/

Sound: This letter sounds like the letter "y" in the word **yellow**.

Forms: This letter has two forms: یـ - ی

- "یـ" is used in the beginning or the middle of a word.
Examples:
beginning: یاس /yǎs/ (jasmine)

middle: مِیمون /mey.mun/ (monkey), آینده /ǎ.yan.de/ (future)

- "ی" is used at the end of a word.
Examples:
end: سعی /saʿy/ (effort), چای /čǎy/ (tea)

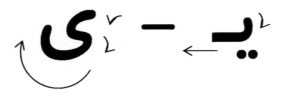

ی ی ی ی ی ی ی

SHORT VOWELS

There are 3 short vowels in the Persian language:

- (´)   /a/

- (ُ)   /o/

- (_)   /e/

They appear in the beginning, in the middle and at the end of a word and they are placed on top of a letter or under it.

Short vowels can not stand alone in the beginning of a word, therefore, they are placed on top of or under the letter ا :   اَ , اُ , اِ

Short vowels can not stand alone at the end of a word, therefore, they change into:

- اُ ⟶ و (at the end or sometimes in the middle of a word)

- اِ ⟶ ه – ـه

- (´) does not appear at the end.

All three original forms of the short vowels: (_) (ُ) (´) can be omitted in writing.

Examples:

دَست ← دست /dast/ (hand)

مُبل ← مبل /mobl/ (sofa)

حِس ← حس /hes/ (sense)

Keep in Mind: If the short vowel is to appear in the beginning of a word, the letter ا stays.

Examples:

آفسانه ← افسانه /af.să.ne/ (fable)

اُتاق ← اتاق /o.tăğ/ (room)

اِلهام ← الهام /el.hăm/ (inspiration)

/a/

Name: /fat.he/

Sound: This vowel sounds like "a" in the word **apple**.

Forms: This vowel appears in two forms: ´ - اَ

- " اَ " is seen in the beginning of a word.

Example:

beginning: اَفسانه /af.să.ne/ (fable)

- " ´ " is placed on top of a letter that is used in the beginning or in the middle of a word.

Examples:

on the top of a letter in the beginning: زَمین /za.min/ (earth)

on the top of a letter in the middle: مادَر /mă.dar/ (mother)

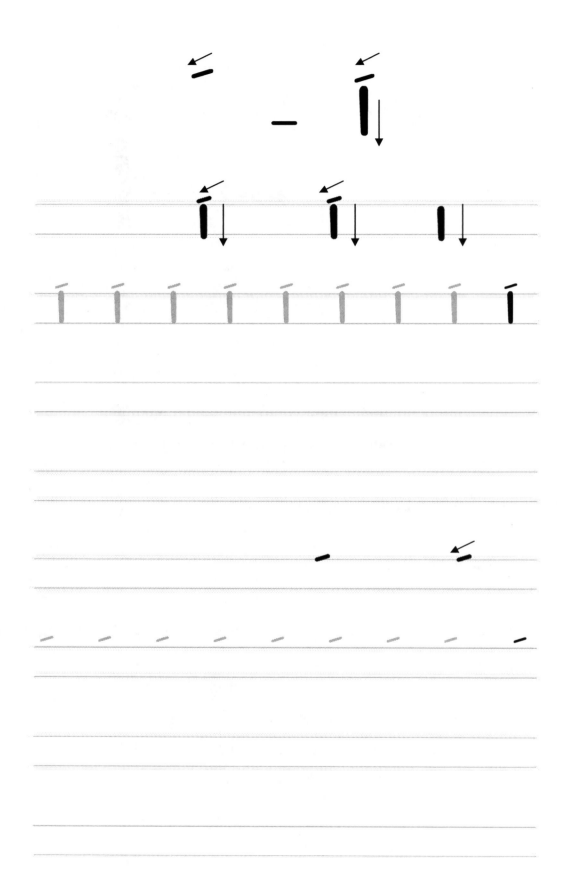

/o/

Name: /zam.me/
Sound: This vowel sounds like "o" in the word **ocean**.
Forms: This vowel appears in three forms: اُ – ُ – و

- "اُ" is seen in the beginning of a word.

Example:

beginning: اُتاق /o.tăğ/ (room)

- " ُ " is placed on top of a letter that is used in the beginning or in the middle of a word.

Examples:

on top of a letter in the beginning: مُبل /mobl/ (sofa)

on top of a letter in the middle: آجُر /ă.jor/ (brick)

- " و " is seen in the middle or at the end of a word.

Examples:

middle: دوشنبه /do.šan.be/ (Monday), موز /moz/ (banana)

end: پرتو /par.to/ (ray), هر دو /har.do/ (both)

Keep in Mind: The vowel " و " only joins the letter preceding it and never the letter following it.

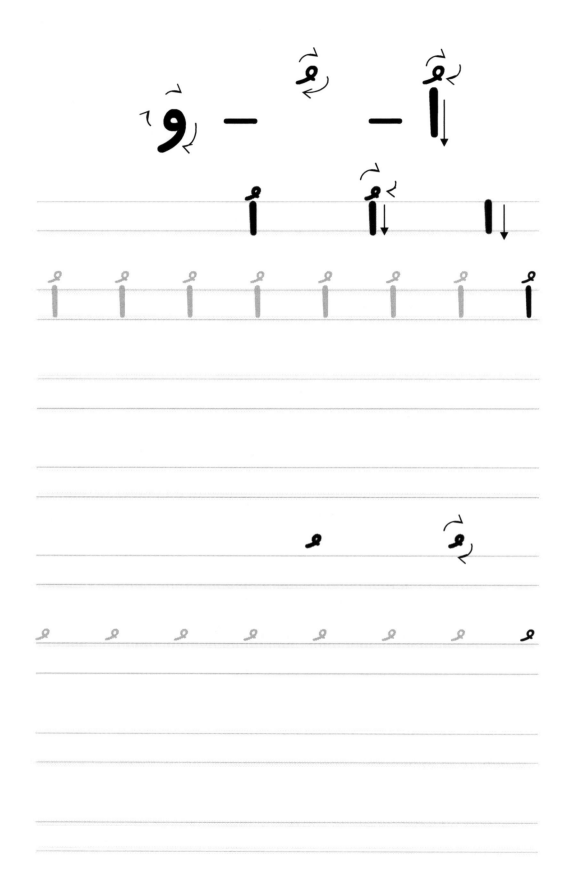

82

ه – ﻪ – ِ – ا

/e/

Name: /kas.re/

Sound: This vowel sounds like "e" in the word **egg**.

Forms: This vowel appears in four forms: ه – ﻪ – ِ – ا

- " ا " is seen in the beginning of a word.

Example:

beginning: الهام /el.hăm/ (inspiration)

- " ِ " is placed under a letter that is used in the beginning or in the

middle of a word.

Examples:

under a letter in the beginning: حِس /hes/ (sense/feeling)

under a letter in the middle: سالِم /să.lem/ (healthy)

- " ﻪ " is seen at the end of a word.

Example:

end: دانه /dă.ne/ (seed)

- " ه " is seen at the end of a word, after one of these 7 letters:

ا, د, ذ, ر, ز, ژ or و .

Example:

end: خنده /ǩan.de/ (laugh)

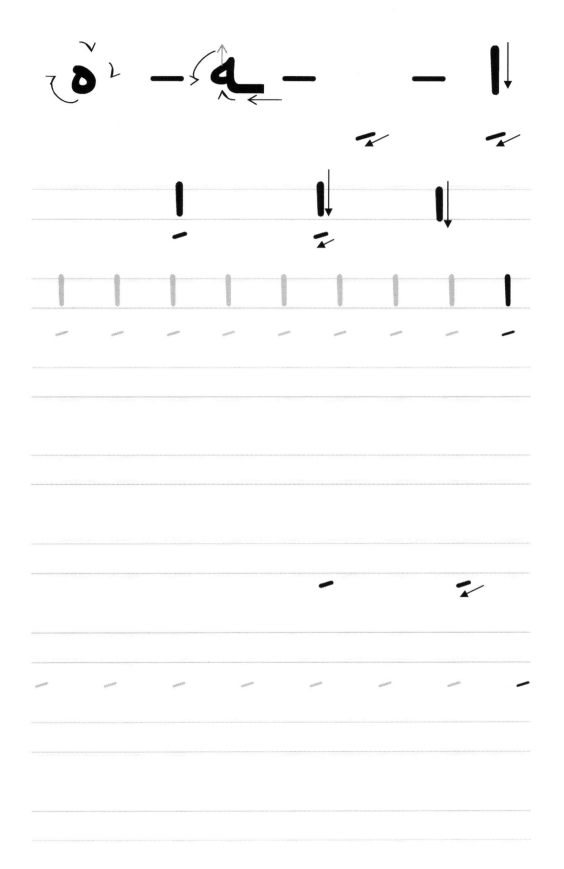

LONG VOWELS

There are 3 long vowels in the Persian language which might share their shapes with specific letters:

ا – آ   /ǎ/

و – او   /u/

ی – ای – یـ – ایـ   /i/

Each have one or more forms depending on their positions in a word.

Keep in Mind: The long vowels can not be omitted in writing.

/ă/

Sound: This vowel sounds like the letter "a" in the word **arm**.

Forms: This vowel has two forms: ‏ا‎ – ‏آ‎

- " ‏آ‎ " is used in the beginning of a word.

Example:

beginning: ‏آب‎ /ăb/ (water)

- " ‏ا‎ " is used in the middle or at the end of a word.

Examples:

middle: ‏باد‎ /băd/ (wind)

end: ‏صدا‎ /se.dă/ (sound), ‏ما‎ /mă/ (we)

Keep in Mind: This long vowel only joins the letter preceding it and never the letter following it.

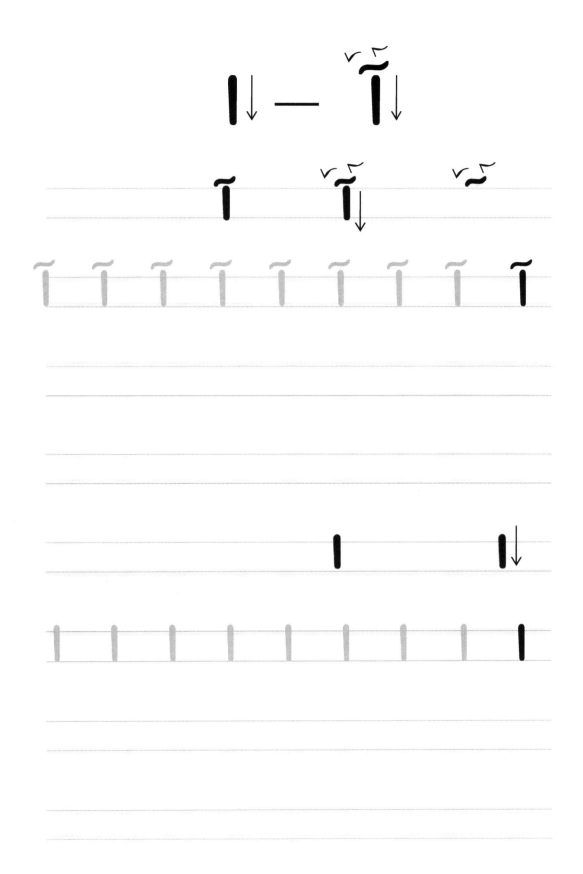

او – و

/u/

Sound: This vowel sounds like "oo" in the middle of the word **root**.

Forms: This vowel has two forms: و – او

- " او " is used in the beginning of a word.

Example:

beginning: اورشلیم /ur.ša.lim/ (Jerusalem)

- " و " is used in the middle or at the end of a word.

Examples:

middle: صورت /su.rat/ (face), زود /zud/ (early)

end: جستجو /jos.te.ju/ (search), ابرو /ab.ru/ (eyebrow)

Keep in Mind: This long vowel only joins the letter preceding it and never the letter following it.

ای - یـ - ای - ی

/i/

Sound: This vowel sounds like "ee" in the middle of the word **seed**.

Forms: This vowel has four forms: ای - ی - یـ - ای

- "ایـ" is used in the beginning of a word.

Example:

beginning: ایران /i.rǎn/ (Iran)

- "یـ" is used in the middle of a word.

Examples:

middle: تیغ /tiğ/ (blade), زیبا /zi.bǎ/ (beautiful)

- "ای" is used at the end of a word after the vowel ه - ـه with /e/ sound.

Examples:

end: خانه ای /kǎ.ne.i/ (a house), پرنده ای /pa.ran.de.i/ (a bird)

- "ی" is used at the end of a word.

Example:

end: بارانی /bǎ.rǎ.ni/ (rainy)

اي - يـ - اي↓ - ىـ - ىـ

اي اب اب↓ اا↓ ا↓

اي اب اب اب اب اب

يـ بـ بـ

يـ يـ يـ يـ يـ يـ

ای ای ای ای ای ای

ای ای ای ای ای ای

ی ی ی ی ی

ی ی ی ی ی ی

ARABIC SIGNS

These are the signs that have entered into the Persian language from Arabic; therefore, the words carrying these signs are Arabic in origin.

There are 3 Arabic signs in the Persian language:

(ّ) (indicates that a letter has to be pronounced twice)

(ً) /an/ (always is placed on top of the letter ا at the end of a word which is an Arabic adverb)

(ع) / ' / (indicates a glottal stop)

ّ

Name: /taš.did/

Sound: This is a "Gemination Mark". It is placed on top of a letter to show that the letter should be pronounced twice.

Forms: This sign has one form: ّ

- " ّ " is placed on top of a letter that is used in the middle or at the end of a word.

Examples:

on top of a letter in the middle: ذرّت /zor.rat/ (corn)

on top of a letter a the end: جوّ /javv/ (atmosphere)

ﺵ   ﺵ   ﺵ

ﺵ   ﺵ   ﺵ   ﺵ   ﺵ   ﺵ   ﺵ

˵

/an/

Name: /tan.vin/

Sound: This Arabic sign is placed on top of the letter ا at the end of a word (an Arabic adverb) and it sounds like "an" at the end of the word **can**.

Forms: This sign has one form: ˵

- " ˵ " is used at the end of a word and is placed on top of the letter ا.

Example:

end: فوراً /fo.ran/ (immediately)

ء

/ʼ/

Name: /ham.ze/

Sound: This Arabic sign is a "glottal stop" like between the syllables of **"uh-oh"**.

Forms: This letter has one form: ء

- " ء " usually is placed on top of one of these three letters:

ـیـ – ی , و , ا .

Examples:

on top of the letter ا in the middle of a word: مأمور /maʼ.mur/ (agent)

next to the letter ا at the end of a word: اشیاء /aš.yăʼ/ (objects)

on top of the letter و in the middle of a word: مؤمن /moʼ.men/ (devout/believer)

on top of the letter ـیـ in the middle of a word: مسئول /mas.ʼul/ (responsible)
(Note: the letter ـیـ turns into ئـ)

on top of the letter ی at the end of a word: شئ /šeyʼ/ (object)

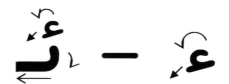

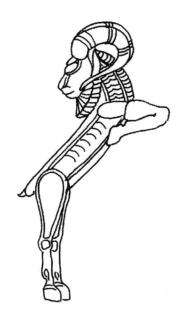

PERSIAN LETTERS
WITH
IDENTICAL SOUNDS

While learning the Persian alphabet, you might find it odd to see different letters with the same sound. This is due to the fact that some letters have entered into the Persian language from Arabic. To make the task of pronouncing the Arabic words easier, the sound of each of these Arabic letters was replaced by the sound of a Persian letter closest to their original sounds. Below is the list of the letters with identical sounds:

‍ـت – ـتـ – ت and ط : these letters sound like the letter "t" in the word **time**.

ـص – صـ , ث – ثـ and س – ـسـ – ـس‍ : these letters sound like the letter "s" in the word **sun**.

ذ , ز , ظ and ضـ – ض : these letters sound like the letter "z" in the word **zoo**.

ح – حـ and ه – هـ – ـهـ – ـه : these letters sound like the letter "h" in the word **happy**.

ق – قـ and غ – غـ – ـغـ – ـغ : these letters sound like the letter " r " in the French word **"merci"**.

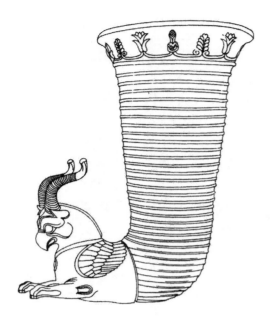

WRITING EXERCISES

Now that you have become familiar with the Persian alphabet and have had a chance to practice writing each letter separately; you can start to practice writing the complete words.

مَن = نْ + مَ

مَن مَن مَن مَن مَن مَن

آ͏َ + تَ + ش = آتَش

آتَش آتَش آتَش آتَش آتَش

کِتاب = ب + اِ + تـ + کِ

کِتاب کِتاب کِتاب کِتاب کِتاب

جيغ = غ + ي + جْ

جيغ   جيغ   جيغ   جيغ   جيغ

صَدَف = ف + دَ + صَّ

صَدَف صَدَف صَدَف صَدَف

طَبل = ل + بـ + طَ

طَبل طَبل طَبل طَبل طَبل

هَـ + ر + گِ + ز = هَرگِز

هَرگِز   هَرگِز   هَرگِز   هَرگِز

111

سَهم = پ + ه + سَ

سَهم سَهم سَهم سَهم سَهم

PERSIAN NUMBERS

Persian numbers are written from left to right.

one	1	١	یک /yek/
two	2	٢	دو /do/
three	3	٣	سه /se/
four	4	٤	چهار /ča.hăr/
five	5	٥	پنج /panj/
six	6	٦	شش /šeš/
seven	7	٧	هفت /haft/
eight	8	٨	هشت /hašt/
nine	9	٩	نه /noh/
ten	10	١٠	ده /dah/

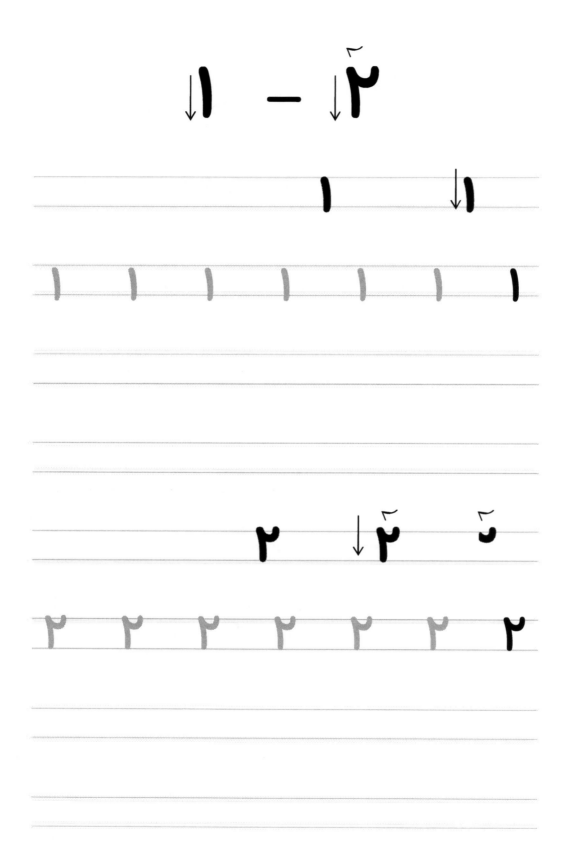

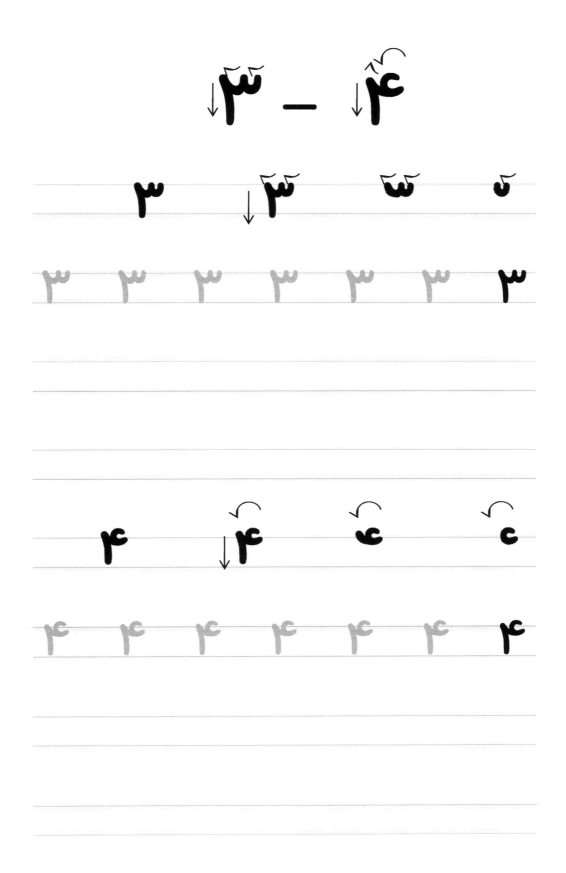

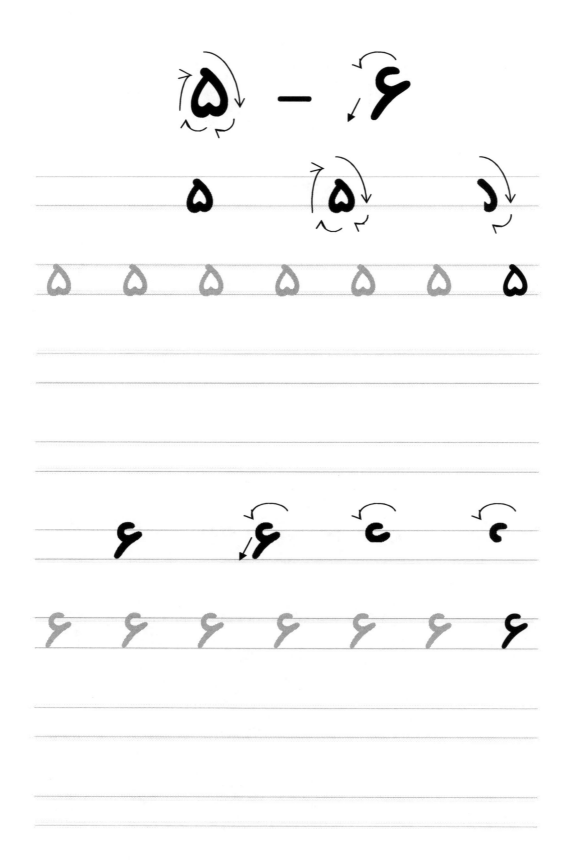

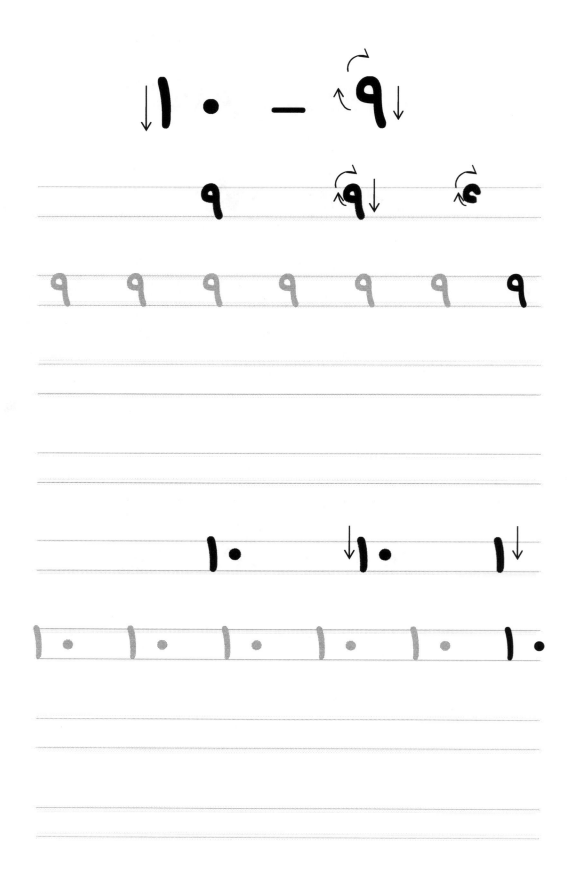

POPULAR PERSIAN FONTS

Similar to English, numerous types of fonts have been created for Persian printing. In this part, you will find the most popular fonts used in creating Persian texts. Most of these fonts are available for download free of charge through various sources on the internet. The name of the fonts are included to facilitate the search, in case you wish to download and use them in your writing. The Persian font used in this book is "Koodak".

Koodak	من دانشجو هستم.
Roya	من دانشجو هستم.
Lotus	من دانشجو هستم.
Time New Roman	من دانشجو هستم.
Badr	من دانشجو هستم.
Mitra	من دانشجو هستم.
Zar	من دانشجو هستم.
Compset	من دانشجو هستم.

Nazanin

من دانشجو هستم.

Yagut

من دانشجو هستم.

IranNastaliq

من دانشجو هستم.

HANDWRITING

It is important to know that in Persian handwriting, the shape of some letters and/or the way they join together to create a word might be different from their printed version. Below, you will find a list of the letters or letter-combinations that defer from their printed versions:

- The shape of two dots in these letters: یـ , ق - ق , ت - تـ can change.

Examples: تیغ →

تیَغ	تیَغ	تیَغ

- The shape of three dots in these letters: ش - شـ , ژ , چ - چـ , ثـ - پ - پـ , ث can change.

Examples: ثلث →

ثلث	ثلث	ثلث

- The letters: س - سـ and ش - شـ can lose their two dents.

Examples: سرسبز → سرسبز   and   شادی → شادی

122

- The shape of the letter ﻬ which is used in the middle of a word, usually changes.

Example: سهم →

- The shape of the letter ﻪ which is used at the end of a word can change.

Example: کوچه →

- The top stroke in the letter ک – ک and the two top strokes in the letter گ – گ usually don't touch their bases.

Examples: بادکنک →  and گندم →

- The vertical line in these letters: ط and ظ usually don't join the base.

Examples: طبل →  and ظالم →

- When the letter ک or گ is followed by the letter ا , it may form a new shape.

Examples: کار →  and گاهی →

123

- When one of these letters: ب – پ – ت – ث – ن – ی is followed by the letter م – ﻤ , the shape of ب – پ – ت – ث – ن – ی may change.

Examples: نمره → نمره , تماشا → تماشا and لیمو → لیمو

- When any of these letters: ج – ﺟ , چ – ﭼ , ح – ﺣ , خ – ﺧ joins another letter, their shapes may change.

Examples: کج → کج , تجارت → تجارت and مجموع → مجموع

HANDWRITING
EXAMPLES &
EXERCISES

In the following pages you will find examples of Persian handwriting. Practice your handwriting by copying the words in the spaces provided.

دانه   دانه   دانه   دانه

تیغ   تیغ   تیغ   تیغ

لازم   لازم   لازم   لازم   لازم

کاج   کاج   کاج   کاج   کاج

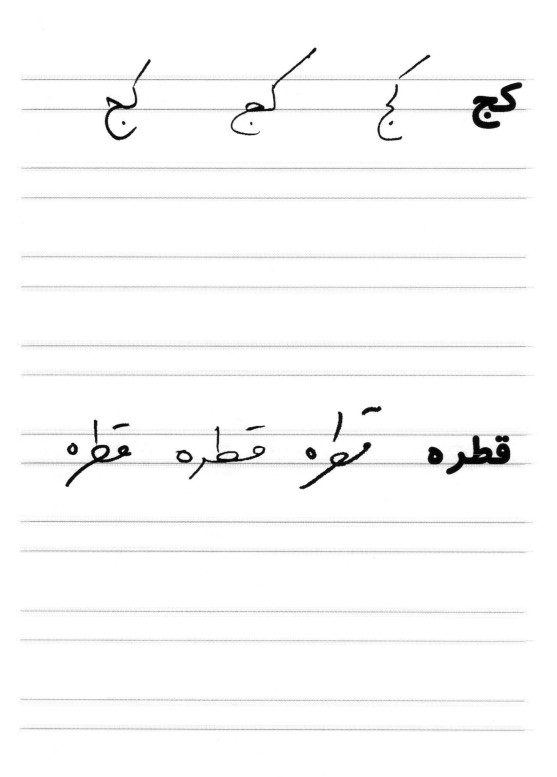

كج   كج   كج   كج

قطره   قطره   قطره   قطره

آرامش آرامش آرامش آرامش آرامش

موزیک موزیک موزیک موزیک موزیک

خانم   خانم   خانم   خانم   خانم

صدا   صدا   صدا   صدا   صدا

شاهین شاهین شاهین شاهین

همیشه همیشه همیشه همیشه

كوچه   كوچه   كوچ   كوچ

سهم   سهم   سهم   سهم   سهم

ثلث   ثلث   ثلث   ثلث

ليمو   ليمو   ليمو   ليمو

گلدان گلدان گلدان **گلدان**

گلدان

چراغ چراغ چراغ **چراغ**

چراغ

معلّم   مُعلّم   مُعلّم   مُعلّم   مُعلّم

سرسبز   سرسبز   سرسبز   سرسبز

دانشگاه دانگاه دانگاه دانشگاه

شما شما شما شتر شما

طناب   طناب   طناب   طناب   طناب

مجموع   مجموع   مجموع   مجموع   مجموع

INDEX OF PERSIAN WORDS USED IN THIS BOOK:

138

انار	pomegranate	68
انگلیسی	English	62
اورشلیم	Jerusalem	90
ایران	Iran	92

ب

باد	wind	10,12,88
بادبادک	kite	60
بادکنک	balloon	60,123
بارانی	rainy	92
بچّه	child	22
بحث	discussion	18
بد	bad	28
برف	snow	56
برق	electricity	58
برگ	leaf	62
بزرگ	big	34

پ

پدر	father	106
پرتو	ray	80
پرنده ای	a bird	92
پسر	boy/son	32,38

ت

تجارت	commerce	20,124
تخت	bed	26
تراش	pencil sharpener	40
تغذیه	nutrition	30
تغییر	change	52
تماشا	viewing	16,123

تیغ	razor blade	92,122,126

ث

ثانیه	second	18
ثلث	one third	133

ج

جستجو	search	90
جنگ	war	20
جوّ	atmosphere	70,96
جوان	young	70
جیغ	scream	53,108

چ

چراغ	lamp	53,134
چرخ	wheel	22

ح

حس	sense/feeling	78,84
حفظ	preservation	48
حلق	throat	24
حیوانات	animals	16

خ

خاص	special	42
خالص	pure	42
خانم	lady	26,130
خانه ای	a house	92
خصوصی	private	42
خط	script/line	47
خنده	laugh	84

د

دانشجو	college student	120,121
دانشگاه	university	72,136
دانه	seed	84,126
دختر	girl/daughter	26
دست	hand	16,28,78
دکتر	doctor	60
دلیل	reason	64
دوشنبه	Monday	81
دونده	runner	70

ذ

ذرّت	corn	30,96

ر

راز	secret	34
رفتار	behavior	56
رقص	dance	58
روز	day	32

ز

زرد	yellow	34
زعفران	saffron	50
زمان	time	68
زمین	earth	79
زود	early	90
زیبا	beautiful	92

ژ

ژاکت	cardigan	36

س

سال	year	64
سالم	healthy	84
سرخ	red	26
سرسبز	freshly green	34,122,135
سفر	trip	56
سنگ	stone	62
سوپ	soup	14
سهم	share	66,72,112,123,132
سیب	apple	38
سیل	flood	64

ش

شادی	happiness/joy	28,122
شاهین	falcon	68,131
شب	night	12
شتر	camel	16
شکل	shape	60
شما	you *pl.*	40,136
شوفاژ	radiator	36
شئ	object	100

ص

صحنه	stage	24
صدا	sound	10,88,130
صدف	shell	42,109
صلح	peace	24
صورت	face	90

ض

ضمیمه	attachment	44

ط

طبل	drum	46,110,123
طناب	rope	68,137

ظ

ظالم	oppressor	123
ظلم	oppression	48

ع

عربی	Arabic	50
عشق	love	58
علم	science	64

غ

غار	cave	53

ف

فارسی	Persian/Farsi	56
فوراً	immediately	98

ق

قاضی	judge	56
قطره	drop	44,126

ک

کاج	pine	20,127
کار	work	32
کاغذ	paper	30
کتاب	book	12,60,107
کج	tilted	20,125,129
کژ	tilted	36
کوچه	alley	22,123,132

کیف	bag	56

گ

گاو	cow	70
گاهی	sometimes	72,123
گچ	chalk	22
گلدان	flowerpot	62,134
گندم	wheat	28,123

ل

لازم	necessary	66,127
لامپ	bulb	14
لحاظ	point of view	48
لیمو	lemon/lime	64,123,133

م

ما	we	10,88
ماچ	kiss	22
مادر	mother	79
مأمور	agent	100
مبل	sofa	12,81
مثبت	positive	18
مجموع	sum	50,124,137
مرثیه	elegy	18
مرد	man	28,32
مرض	sickness	44
مریض	sick	44
مژه	eyelash	36
مس	copper	38
مسئول	responsible	100
مضمون	content	44

مطّلع	Knowledgeable	50
مظهر	symbol	48
معلّم	teacher	50,135
من	I	66,105,120,121
موز	banana	81
موزیک	music	34,129
مؤمن	devout/believer	100
میمون	monkey	76

ن

نشاط	happiness/joy	46
نقطه	dot	58
نمره	number/grade	68,123
نه	nine	72,113

و

واضح	clear	44
ورزش	sport	70
وظیفه	task	48

ه

هر دو	both	81
هرگز	never	72,111
هستم	am	120,121
همیشه	forever/always	66,131

ی

یاس	jasmine	38,75
یخ	ice	26

Related Titles By Nazanin Mirsadeghi

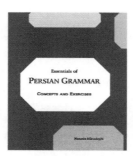

Essentials of
Persian Grammar:
Concepts and Exercises

100
Irregular Persian Verbs
(Fully Conjugated in the Most Common Tenses)

1000 +
Most Useful
Persian Words

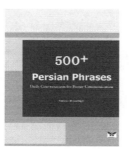

500 +
Persian Phrases
(Daily Conversations for Better Communication)

100
Persian Verbs
(Fully Conjugated in the Most Common Tenses)

Laugh & Learn
Persian Idioms

Bahar Books

To Learn More About Bahar Books' Publications, Visit:

www.baharbooks.com

Made in the USA
San Bernardino, CA
02 October 2015